FEDERALISTS

AND

ANTI-FEDERALISTS

NATHAN MILOSZEWSKI

PowerKiDS
press

New York

Published in 2020 by The Rosen Publishing Group, Inc.
29 East 21st Street, New York, NY 10010

First Edition

Editor: Jane Katirgis
Book Design: Tanya Dellaccio

Photo Credits: Cover (left) GraphicaArtis/Archive Photos/Getty Images; cover (right), pp. 5 (constitutional convention), 19, 21 Fotosearch/Archive Photos/Getty Images; p. 5 (map) Bettmann/Getty Images; p. 7 https://upload.wikimedia.org/wikipedia/commons/9/9d/Scene_at_the_Signing_of_the_Constitution_of_the_United_States.jpg; p. 9 (Articles of Confederation) Courtesy of Our Documents; p. 9 (drafting of the Articles of Confederation) artnana/Shutterstock.com; p. 11 (Alexander Hamilton) https://upload.wikimedia.org/wikipedia/commons/0/05/Alexander_Hamilton_portrait_by_John_Trumbull_1806.jpg; p. 11 (Ben Franklin) https://upload.wikimedia.org/wikipedia/commons/2/25/Benjamin_Franklin_by_Joseph_Duplessis_1778.jpg; p. 11 (John Adams) https://upload.wikimedia.org/wikipedia/commons/9/9e/Johnadamsvp.flipped.jpg; p. 11 (James Madison) https://upload.wikimedia.org/wikipedia/commons/1/1d/James_Madison.jpg; p. 11 (John Jay) https://upload.wikimedia.org/wikipedia/commons/7/72/John_Jay_%28Gilbert_Stuart_portrait%29.jpg; p. 13 (George Mason) https://upload.wikimedia.org/wikipedia/commons/b/bb/George_Mason_portrait.jpg; p. 13 (James Monroe) https://upload.wikimedia.org/wikipedia/commons/9/95/James_Monroe_White_House_portrait_1819.gif; p. 13 (Samuel Adams) https://upload.wikimedia.org/wikipedia/commons/8/89/J_S_Copley_-_Samuel_Adams.jpg; p. 13 (Patrick Henry) https://upload.wikimedia.org/wikipedia/commons/e/ea/Patrick_henry.JPG; p. 17 Pigrox/Shutterstock.com; p. 23 (illustration) Universal History Archive/Universal Images Group/Getty Images; p. 23 (The Federalist) https://upload.wikimedia.org/wikipedia/commons/c/c7/The_Federalist_%281st_ed%2C_1788%2C_vol_I%2C_title_page%29_-_02.jpg; p. 25 (top) Alan Budman/Shutterstock.com; p. 25 (bottom) f11photo/Shutterstock.com; p. 27 (James Madison) Everett Historical/Shutterstock.com; p. 27 (Bill of Rights) https://upload.wikimedia.org/wikipedia/commons/7/79/Bill_of_Rights_Pg1of1_AC.jpg; p. 29 https://upload.wikimedia.org/wikipedia/commons/5/59/Kings_County_Courthouse_%28Kingston_Free_Library%29.jpg.

Cataloging-in-Publication Data
Names: Miloszewski, Nathan.
Title: Federalists and anti-federalists / Nathan Miloszewski.
Description: New York : PowerKids Press, 2019. | Series: Opponents in American history | Includes glossary and index.
Identifiers: ISBN 9781538345405 (pbk.) | ISBN 9781538343678 (library bound) | ISBN 9781538345412 (6 pack)
Subjects: LCSH: Federalist–Juvenile literature. | Constitutional history–United States–Juvenile literature. | Federal government–United States–History–18th century–Juvenile literature. | United States–Politics and government–1783-1789–Juvenile literature.
Classification: LCC KF4515.M556 2019 | DDC 342.7302'4–dc23

Manufactured in the United States of America

CPSIA Compliance Information: Batch #CSPK19. For Further Information contact Rosen Publishing, New York, New York at 1-800-237-9932

CONTENTS

AFTER THE REVOLUTIONARY WAR

Picture yourself in the mid-1780s. The American Revolutionary War was over. After declaring independence from Great Britain in 1776 and winning the war, the 13 colonies were now a new nation known as the United States.

The Confederation Congress was the governing body created in 1781 by the Articles of Confederation, the young nation's first constitution. It soon became clear to many leaders, however, that the country needed a stronger constitution.

In 1787, **delegates** from the 13 states met for the Constitutional Convention in Philadelphia, Pennsylvania. At first, they met to improve the Articles, but the focus soon turned to creating a new constitution for the United States. As this new constitution took shape, however, two groups arose in support of and against it: the Federalists and the anti-Federalists.

CONSTITUTIONAL CONVENTION, 1787

THE ORIGINAL 13 BRITISH COLONIES IN NORTH AMERICA BECAME THE FIRST 13 STATES.

THE FEDERALISTS

The term "Federalist" refers to people who supported the U.S. Constitution created in 1787 and worked for its **ratification**. The term also refers to people who were members of the Federalist Party, which formed in 1791 and supported a strong central government.

Federalists wanted a stronger national **republic** with specific powers. They wanted the federal government to have some power over the individual states. They also said the government should have more power to collect taxes from the people and make decisions for the country as a whole. Federalists supported a national bank and strong central financial policies. They tended to want more industry in the nation, and they didn't think a separate bill of rights was needed.

THE
ANTI-FEDERALISTS

Can you imagine the United States without the Constitution? You might be studying the Articles of Confederation as the country's governing **document** today if anti-Federalist ideas had won over the country.

The Articles of Confederation, America's first constitution, was created by the Continental Congress, adopted in 1777, and ratified by all 13 states by 1781. The anti-Federalists preferred the Articles because that constitution created a weak central government while loosely banding the states together. Many did think the Articles needed to be improved, but they didn't want a new constitution.

Many anti-Federalists believed in states' rights. They thought the individual states and local governments should have more power than the federal government. They felt that the new U.S. Constitution gave the federal government too much power, which might threaten personal freedoms.

Drafting the Articles of Confederation

York Town, Pennsylvania 1777 **13**c USA

REVISING THE ARTICLES OF CONFEDERATION

By 1787, U.S. leaders decided to hold a convention to revise, or change, the Articles of Confederation. The federal government didn't have enough power to deal with other countries without the states blocking it and couldn't regulate trade or taxes. The states also had trouble working together without a strong federal government. The original plan to simply revise the Articles was quickly scrapped in favor of creating a new constitution.

FAMOUS FEDERALISTS

There were famous Founding Fathers on both sides of the constitutional **debate**. On the Federalist side, Alexander Hamilton may be the most well-known Founding Father. He became the first secretary of the treasury under President Washington and later founded the Federalist Party. John Adams was the first vice president and America's second president. He was in Great Britain at the time the Constitution was created, but he later joined Hamilton's Federalist Party.

Benjamin Franklin was known for his many inventions and as a signer of three important American documents: the Declaration of Independence, the Treaty of Paris that ended the Revolution, and the U.S. Constitution. James Madison (the fourth U.S. president) and John Jay (first chief justice of the Supreme Court) were also supporters of the U.S. Constitution.

JOHN
JAY

JAMES
MADISON

JAY, MADISON, AND HAMILTON
PUBLISHED A SERIES OF ESSAYS
SUPPORTING FEDERALIST IDEALS.
THESE ESSAYS BECAME KNOWN
AS "THE FEDERALIST PAPERS."

JOHN
ADAMS

ALEXANDER
HAMILTON

BENJAMIN
FRANKLIN

11

FAMOUS
ANTI-FEDERALISTS

Patrick Henry of Virginia was one of the leaders of the anti-Federalists. He was an important leader during the American Revolution and the state of Virginia's first governor. Henry was concerned the U.S. Constitution didn't give the states or the U.S. people enough rights. Samuel Adams was a cousin of another Founding Father, John Adams, and a leader during the Revolution.

George Mason of Virginia, a delegate to the Constitutional Convention, wrote the Virginia Declaration of Rights, which later became a model for the U.S. Bill of Rights. He refused to sign the U.S. Constitution. James Monroe served as a U.S. senator for Virginia, helped to negotiate the Louisiana Purchase to buy land from France, and became the fifth president of the United States.

ON THE MONEY

Alexander Hamilton's face is on the $10 bill, Thomas Jefferson is on the nickel and the rare $2 bill, and George Washington is on the $1 bill and the quarter. Alexander Hamilton is just one of two Founding Fathers who never became president but still appears on current U.S. paper money still in circulation. Can you think of the other one? The answer: Benjamin Franklin ($100 bill).

PATRICK HENRY

JAMES MONROE

SAMUEL ADAMS

GEORGE MASON

JOHN ADAMS WAS A FEDERALIST, AND HIS OLDER COUSIN SAMUEL ADAMS WAS AN ANTI-FEDERALIST. HOWEVER, SAMUEL ADAMS LATER SUPPORTED THE CONSTITUTION AFTER THE BILL OF RIGHTS WAS ADDED.

CITY VS. COUNTRY

Where people lived and how they made a living were other factors explaining why Federalists and anti-Federalists had different views on how the country should be run. Federalist supporters often lived in urban areas, or cities. They tended to be what we might call "white collar" professionals today. Federalists tended to be educated businessmen, bankers, and lawyers who felt that a strong central government should be regulating the economy.

Anti-Federalist supporters mostly lived in rural areas, out in the country. They were often farmers or "blue collar" workers who lived in small towns and villages. They believed their state and local governments could manage themselves without the interference of a large federal government.

TAKE A LOOK AT THE CORE BELIEFS AND TRAITS OF EACH SIDE DURING THE CONSTITUTION DEBATE. WHICH SIDE WOULD YOU BE ON?

WOULD YOU BE A FEDERALIST OR AN ANTI-FEDERALIST?

FEDERALIST

- STRONG FEDERAL GOVERNMENT

- PERSONAL RIGHTS IMPLIED BY THE CONSTITUTION

- OFTEN LIVED IN URBAN AREAS

- BUSINESS AND INDUSTRY

- SUPPORTED THE U.S. CONSTITUTION

- CHECKS AND BALANCES WITH THREE BRANCHES OF GOVERNMENT (EXECUTIVE, LEGISLATIVE, JUDICIAL) TO LIMIT POWER

ANTI-FEDERALIST

- STRONG STATE GOVERNMENT, WEAK FEDERAL GOVERNMENT

- DEMANDED A SEPARATE BILL OF RIGHTS

- OFTEN LIVED IN RURAL AREAS

- AGRARIAN (FARMING) SOCIETY

- WANTED TO REVISE ARTICLES OF CONFEDERATION

- THOUGHT THE FEDERAL GOVERNMENT WAS BEING GIVEN TOO MUCH POWER

CONSTITUTIONAL CONVENTION

When representatives from 12 states (Rhode Island refused to take part) gathered in Philadelphia, Pennsylvania, for the Constitutional Convention, there were many different things to discuss. The delegates worked for five months before they approved the U.S. Constitution, a feat that took a lot of compromise and debate.

After the Revolutionary War, many Americans were afraid their new government might become too powerful. Having just gained independence from Great Britain, people didn't want to give up personal rights and freedoms again. So, the issue of how the unique interests of different states would be represented in Congress was a topic of great debate. Delegates from small states didn't agree with delegates from large states about how the states should be represented. People proposed a number of plans based on different factors.

WHERE IT HAPPENED— INDEPENDENCE HALL

The early U.S. government used the Pennsylvania State House in Philadelphia during the Revolution and the years afterward. This is the site where the Declaration of Independence was signed and where the U.S. Constitution was debated and signed. Today it's known as Independence Hall. Fifty-five delegates took part in the Constitutional Convention and thirty-nine signed the finished document.

HEAD TO HEAD

James Madison is known as the "Father of the Constitution" because of his important role, or part, in writing the document and working toward its ratification.

17

THE CONNECTICUT COMPROMISE

Constitutional Convention delegates from states with a lot of people wanted representation in the new Congress to be based on population, which would put small states at a serious disadvantage. Small states wanted representation to be even no matter what the population was. Both sides refused to back down. Fortunately, two representatives from Connecticut came up with a two-part solution. It was called the Connecticut Compromise.

Under this compromise, the new Congress would have two houses. Representation in the House of Representatives would be based on a state's population. Representation in the Senate would be two senators per state, no matter the population size. In a way, this compromise saved the Constitution—but there were still battles left to fight for the document's supporters.

THE POLITICAL PROCESS IS RARELY PRETTY. A CARTOON
PUBLISHED IN 1798 SHOWS A FIGHT IN CONGRESS BETWEEN
REPRESENTATIVES FROM VERMONT AND CONNECTICUT.

HEAD TO HEAD

*The U.S. Constitution is the oldest
national constitution that's still being
used today. It is also the shortest.*

Thirty-nine delegates to the Constitutional Convention signed the finished U.S. Constitution on September 17, 1787. After that, at least nine of the 13 individual states had to ratify it. This is where the battles between the Federalists and the anti-Federalists really heated up.

Anti-Federalists opposed the ratification of the U.S. Constitution. Delegates such as George Mason were concerned that it would create a federal government that was too powerful and that it didn't contain a list of the people's rights.

The anti-Federalists argued against the new constitution at the state ratifying conventions, which were official meetings required so that state residents could debate about the document. Anti-Federalists also criticized the Constitution by saying it was illegal, served only special interests, and gave the federal government too much power

REDEUNT SATURNIA REGNA.
On the erection of the Eleventh PILLAR of the great National DOME, we beg leave most sincerely to felicitate " OUR DEAR COUNTRY."

Rise it will.

The foundation good—it may yet be SAVED.

The FEDERAL EDIFICE.

ELEVEN STARS, in quick succession rise—
ELEVEN COLUMNS strike our wond'ring eyes,
Soon o'er the *whole*, shall swell the beauteous DOME,
COLUMBIA's boast—and FREEDOM's hallow'd home.
Here shall the ARTS in glorious splendour shine !
And AGRICULTURE give her stores divine !
COMMERCE refin'd, dispense us more than gold,
And this new world, teach WISDOM to the old—

THIS ILLUSTRATION FROM THE AUGUST 2, 1788, EDITION OF THE *MASSACHUSETTS SENTINEL* SHOWS THE RATIFICATION PROGRESS. HERE, NEW HAMPSHIRE IS THE NINTH STATE TO RATIFY, WITH VIRGINIA AND NEW YORK POSSIBLY NEXT—AND PROBLEMS BEYOND.

HEAD TO HEAD

On September 28, 1787, Congress sent the U.S. Constitution to the states for ratification. On December 7, 1787, Delaware became the first state to ratify it. It did so by a unanimous vote of 30–0.

WHAT IF A STATE DIDN'T RATIFY?

Historians have wondered what would have happened if one of the states never ratified the Constitution. Would they have been left out of the Union and be separate from the rest of the country? There was no plan in place had that happened. The Founding Fathers wrote the Constitution with the expectation that all states would eventually agree to it.

THE FEDERALIST PAPERS

The Federalists weren't going to stand still and let the anti-Federalists sink the Constitution, however. In 1787 and 1788, Founding Fathers Alexander Hamilton, James Madison, and John Jay wrote "The Federalist papers," 85 essays that explained the Constitution and promoted its ratification. These essays were originally published in New York newspapers under the **pseudonym** "Publius."

The essays were meant to help influence public opinion about the U.S. Constitution, but they served another important purpose as well. The organized, printed form of their arguments showed the Federalists as much more organized than the anti-Federalists. The Federalists had the answers ready to defend their side.

Compared to the Federalist movement, the anti-Federalists weren't as well organized or prepared. This hurt their chances during the state ratifying conventions.

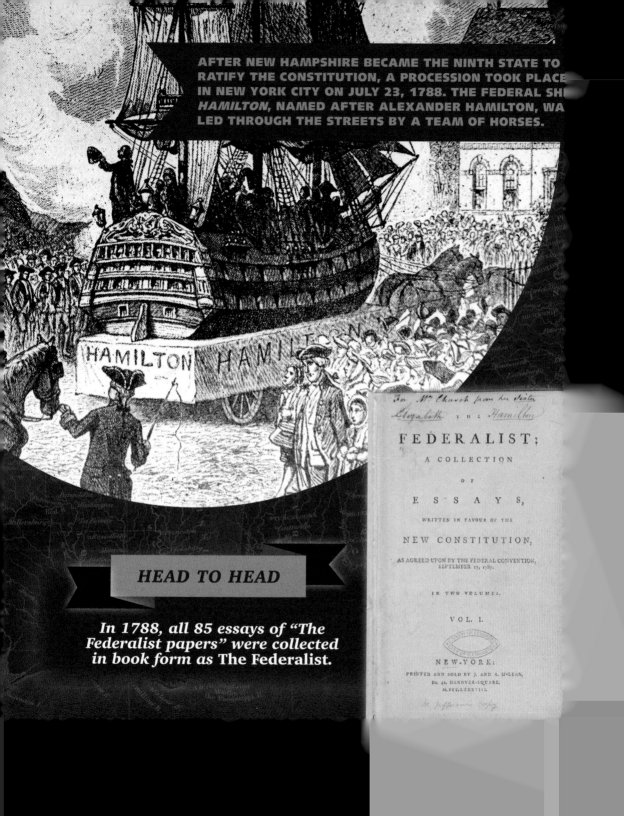

AFTER NEW HAMPSHIRE BECAME THE NINTH STATE TO RATIFY THE CONSTITUTION, A PROCESSION TOOK PLACE IN NEW YORK CITY ON JULY 23, 1788. THE FEDERAL SHI*HAMILTON*, NAMED AFTER ALEXANDER HAMILTON, WA LED THROUGH THE STREETS BY A TEAM OF HORSES.

HEAD TO HEAD

In 1788, all 85 essays of "The Federalist papers" were collected in book form as The Federalist.

THE

FEDERALIST;

A COLLECTION

OF

E S S A Y S,

WRITTEN IN FAVOUR OF THE

NEW CONSTITUTION,

AS AGREED UPON BY THE FEDERAL CONVENTION,
SEPTEMBER 17, 1787.

IN TWO VOLUMES.

VOL. I.

NEW-YORK:

PRINTED AND SOLD BY J. AND A. M^cLEAN,
No. 41, HANOVER-SQUARE.
M.DCC.LXXXVIII.

PRESS AND THE
POST OFFICE

Both Federalists and anti-Federalists often hid their identities when their views were printed in newspapers. They wanted readers to focus on the ideas and not the authors. Also, it was unsafe to reveal which side you were on in certain parts of the country, especially for anti-Federalists.

Some newspaper printers stayed **unbiased**, but many took sides in the debate, printing more Federalist or anti-Federalist material. In July 1788, a mob **vandalized** the print shop of the anti-Federalist printer of the *New York Journal*. Many anti-Federalists also didn't trust the post office. They accused Federalists with interfering with the mail and claimed their letters and anti-Federalist newspapers weren't being delivered. Anti-Federalists tried not to use the official post office if they didn't have to.

POWER OF THE PEN

Hamilton, Jay, and Madison weren't the only ones writing in support of or against ratification. They're just the most famous today. Many people took up a pen, including New York Governor George Clinton, who wrote anti-Federalist essays under the name "Cato." Writer Mercy Otis Warren also opposed ratification and penned essays about it.

BENJAMIN FRANKLIN WAS THE FIRST POSTMASTER GENERAL
UNDER THE CONSTITUTIONAL CONGRESS. THE B. FREE FRANKLIN
POST OFFICE AND MUSEUM IN PHILADELPHIA, PENNSYLVANIA,
IS THE ONLY COLONIAL-THEMED POST OFFICE OPERATED BY THE
UNITED STATES POSTAL SERVICE TODAY.

ESTABLISHING A
BILL OF RIGHTS

Although George Mason and others had requested a bill of rights in the new U.S. Constitution, the Federalists considered this unnecessary. Many of the existing state constitutions already **guaranteed** some rights, and the checks and balances listed in the Constitution limited the federal government enough, they said. Federalists also noted that creating a particular list of rights might actually limit people to just those rights.

However, in February 1788, Massachusetts agreed to ratification—but only with the **stipulation** that a bill of rights be added to the Constitution. This Massachusetts Compromise paved the way for more states to ratify the Constitution. Four other states did so with a bill of rights as a condition. On June 21, 1788, New Hampshire became the ninth state to ratify the Constitution, making it official.

HEAD TO HEAD

The Virginia Declaration of Rights, written by George Mason, is the model on which James Madison based the U.S. Bill of Rights.

JAMES MADISON WAS A FEDERALIST, BUT HE AGREED THAT A BILL OF RIGHTS WAS NEEDED IF THE U.S. CONSTITUTION WAS GOING TO BE RATIFIED.

THE BILL OF RIGHTS

James Madison wrote 19 amendments for the Constitution. Congress adopted 12 on September 25, 1789, and sent them to the states for ratification. Ten of these amendments were ratified by December 15, 1791, and became the U.S. Bill of Rights. These amendments protect the freedoms of speech and religion and many other rights. One of the two remaining proposed amendments was ratified in 1992 as the 27th Amendment.

THE LAST STATE
TO RATIFY

After New Hampshire, Virginia, New York, and North Carolina gradually ratified the constitution. Rhode Island was the 13th and final state to ratify, living up to its "Rogue Island" nickname. The state had refused to send delegates to the Constitutional Convention at all.

The U.S. Constitution was rejected 11 times in Rhode Island. The governor of the state told Congress that the state's leaders were still concerned that the federal government would have too much power.

Rhode Island finally ratified the Constitution on May 29, 1790, almost two years after it was officially ratified and more than a year after George Washington became president. Ratification only passed by two votes. The state suggested 21 amendments when it did so.

FASHIONABLY LATE

When Rhode Island finally ratified the Constitution, it meant the state could participate in the federal government. So, on August 31, 1790, more than a year after the first Congress met under the new Constitution, Rhode Island's only representative, Benjamin Bourne, arrived in Philadelphia. It was reported that he was "fashionably late," staying true to the state's lack of urgency.

THIS IS RHODE ISLAND'S WASHINGTON COUNTY COURTHOUSE. THE STATE ONLY RATIFIED THE CONSTITUTION AFTER THE UNITED STATES THREATENED A TRADE **EMBARGO**.

HEAD TO HEAD

Rhode Island wasn't the only state that lagged behind in ratification. North Carolina ratified the U.S. Constitution only six months earlier, in November 1789.

29

THE LEGACY

Both Federalist and anti-Federalist contributions have had a lasting **legacy** and strong effects on U.S. political opinions. People still read the essays Federalists and anti-Federalists wrote and talk about the balance between states' rights and the power of the federal government.

Forcing the first Congress to include a bill of rights was the single greatest victory of the anti-Federalists. The Federalists, however, succeeded in creating a strong government that could do what it had to as it represented the United States before the world.

The anti-Federalists and the Federalists marked the very beginnings of the U.S. two-party system. While there was no anti-Federalist party, Thomas Jefferson created the Republican Party (later the Democratic-Republicans) in 1792 to counteract Hamilton's Federalist Party. In many ways, the debate continues today.

GLOSSARY

debate: An argument or public discussion. Also, to argue or discuss something.

delegate: A person sent to a meeting or convention to represent others.

document: A formal piece of writing.

embargo: A government order that limits trade.

guarantee: To make a formal promise that certain conditions will be fulfilled.

legacy: The lasting effect of a person or thing.

pseudonym: A name used instead of a real name.

ratification: The act of officially approving something.

republic: A country governed by elected representatives and an elected leader.

stipulation: Something that is demanded or required as part of an agreement.

unbiased: Not having a tendency to believe that some people or ideas are better than others.

vandalize: To damage or destroy something on purpose.

INDEX

WEBSITES

Due to the changing nature of Internet links, PowerKids Press has developed an online list of websites related to the subject of this book. This site is updated regularly. Please use this link to access the list: www.powerkidslinks.com/oiah/federalists